Beginning to END
Grass To Milk

A Buddy Book

by

Julie Murray

ABDO
Publishing Company

VISIT US AT
www.abdopublishing.com

Published by ABDO Publishing Company, 4940 Viking Drive, Edina, Minnesota 55435.

Printed in the United States.

Coordinating Series Editor: Sarah Tieck
Contributing Editor: Michael P. Goecke
Graphic Design: Maria Hosley
Cover Photograph: Photos.com
Interior Photographs/Illustrations: Business Wire via Getty Images (page 19), Clipart.com, Darren McCollester/Newsmakers/Getty Images (page 17), Media Bakery, Minden Pictures, Photos.com

Library of Congress Cataloging-in-Publication Data

Murray, Julie, 1969-
Grass to milk / Julie Murray.
p. cm. — (Beginning to end)
Includes bibliographical references and index.
ISBN-13: 978-1-59679-837-3
ISBN-10: 1-59679-837-8
1. Dairying—Juvenile literature. 2. Milk—Juvenile literature. 3. Cows—Juvenile literature. I. Title.

SF239.5.M87 2007
637'.1—dc22

2006019899

Table Of Contents

Where Does Milk Come From?

Many people like to drink milk. Milk is also used to make products such as cheese and ice cream. Some people even use milk in bath and beauty products. Do you know where milk comes from?

Cheese, butter, and sour cream are some of the dairy products that people eat.

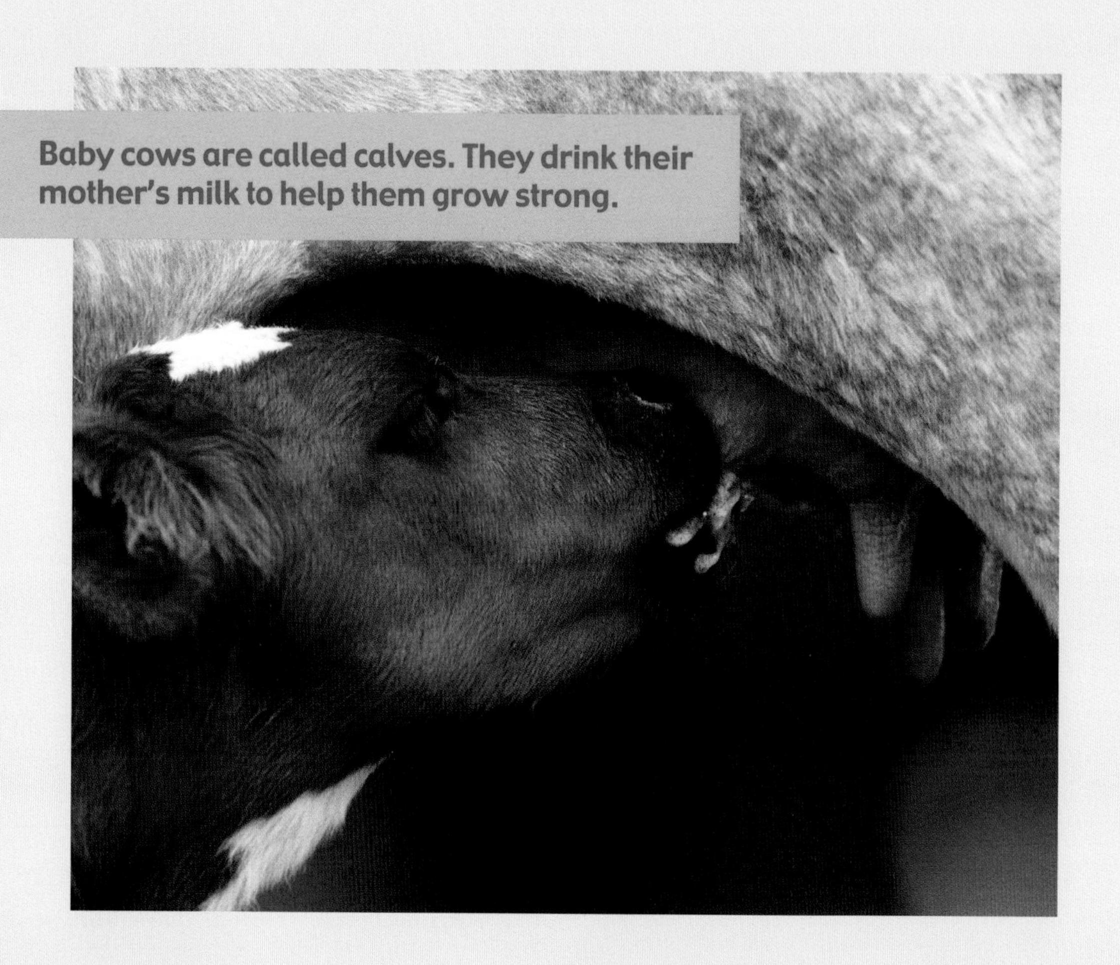
Baby cows are called calves. They drink their mother's milk to help them grow strong.

Milk is a natural product. **Mammals** that have recently had babies make milk. Their bodies produce milk to feed their babies.

Look at a jug of milk. The label says what kind of milk it is. Some grocery stores sell goat's milk. But, most people buy milk that comes from cows.

Milk is refrigerated at stores.

A Starting Point

Cows are large animals. They live on farms throughout the world. Cows **graze** in fields of grass, and eat hay, corn, and oats. Eating these foods helps cows to grow strong and healthy.

Some cows are raised for their meat. These cows are called beef cows. Steaks and hamburgers are some of the foods made from beef cows.

Cows eat grass in fields.

Other farmers raise cows for their milk. This milk is used to make dairy products. That's why these cows are called dairy cows. Butter, cheese, and yogurt are some of the foods that come from dairy cows.

A Natural Process

A cow has an **udder** that hangs down near its back legs. This is where its milk is made and stored. A cow's body makes milk after it has a baby. Then, the calf drinks milk from its mother's udder.

Cows can make up to 10 gallons (38 l) of milk each day.

Most calves drink milk from their mothers for a couple of days. After that, farmers feed the calves. Then, the farmers can sell the milk from the mother cows.

FUN Facts

Did you know...

... Holstein cows make the most milk of any kind of cow.

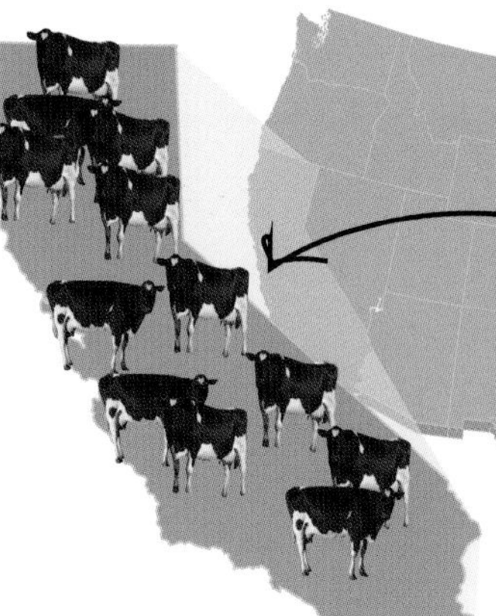

... California and Wisconsin are the top milk producers in the U.S.

... A cow's stomach has four parts. Because of this, its body uses food in a different way. The cow's body breaks down food in stages. After a cow swallows food, the food comes back up again. It is called cud. The cow chews the cud and swallows again.

... Milk is considered the most **nourishing** of all foods.

Milking Time

Farmers must milk their cows to get milk. Dairy cows are milked twice each day.

Some farmers only have a few cows. These farmers can milk their cows by hand.

Other dairy farms have hundreds of cows. Most large dairy farms have milking machines to milk cows more quickly.

People can milk cows by hand.

To milk a cow by hand, a farmer squeezes the **teats** on a cow's **udder**. This makes the milk squirt out. Milking machines use a similar process to get the cow's milk.

From Udder To Table

After milking, farmers store the fresh milk in special tanks. These tanks keep the milk cold, so that it does not spoil. This helps make sure the milk is safe for people to use.

Later, a truck picks up the cold milk from the dairy farm. Then, the truck brings it to a dairy factory.

At dairy farms, milk is stored in large tanks. These tanks help keep the milk cool, so it is safe to drink.

People drink milk that is **pasteurized**. When milk is pasteurized, it is heated for a very short time. This helps clean the milk by killing any **bacteria**.

Next, machines at the dairy put the milk into containers. Some of the milk is ready for drinking. And, some of the milk is made into other products, such as cheese or butter.

Machines pasteurize milk. This process makes the milk safe for people to drink.

As a snack, many people eat cookies with milk.

After milk is bottled and **pasteurized**, it is sold to grocery stores. People can buy the milk, and take it home to drink.

Next time you pour milk into a glass, think about its journey from **udder** to table!

Can You Guess?

Q: Where does butter come from?

A: Butterfat

Q: Which states in the United States have the most dairy cows?

A: Wisconsin and California

Important Words

bacteria very small organisms that can grow in food and other places. Bacteria can make people sick.

graze to eat.

mammal most living things that belong to this special group have hair, give birth to live babies, and make milk to feed their babies.

nourish to provide what is needed for life.

pasteurization a special process for cleaning milk.

teats the part of an udder where milk comes out.

udder the body part of a cow that makes and holds milk.

Web Sites

To learn more, visit ABDO Publishing Company on the World Wide Web. Web site links about this topic are featured on our Book Links page. These links are routinely monitored and updated to provide the most current information available.

www.abdopublishing.com

Index